Words I Couldn't Say

Dani Lyons

BookLeaf Publishing

India | USA | UK

Presentation by *BookLeaf Publishing*

Web: www.bookleafpub.com

E-mail: info@bookleafpub.com

ISBN: 9789357448482

First edition 2022

DEDICATION

To the girl who is just now figuring out how to put herself first, you're doing great.

ACKNOWLEDGEMENT

To my family, thank you for always believing in me and supporting my journey.
To my friends, thank you for laughing with me, crying with me, and knowing exactly how to pick me up when I'm down.

PREFACE

When we hear mice squeak
We make jokes about how quiet they sound
But perhaps it came from deep within
Like when a lion roars
Maybe the mouse roars too

Even if your voice shakes, say the things that
will bring you peace.

All wounds heal if you let them

Someone once said to me
"If you don't heal what hurt you,
you'll bleed on people who didn't cut you."
This hit so close to home
I went to my room to hide
And watched the blood drip from my wrists
Down to my fingertips
And land on my feet

I wish your memories left with you

You can miss someone
And still not want them back in your life
Because at the end of the day
It's your memory knocking on my door
Not you

Remnants of your exit

You're not just the aching of a broken heart
You're the deja vu while driving around town
You're the cold, empty space in my bed
You're the shoes I got for my birthday
And the clothes you never came back for
You're the painful silence where there used to be
laughter
You're the song I have to change every time it
comes on
You're the name I avoid saying when telling
stories
You're also the reason why I'm not the same
person anymore

Always be your
mini-me

People always ask who I look more alike
With a smile I say neither
I've always proudly worn it on my sleeve how
different I am
But when they ask who I'm more alike
I'd sigh and say you
I never wanted to even have the slightest
resemblance to someone
But the truth is
I could not be more like you
The way we think of the same joke
And laugh when the other person gets it out first
Or the way we value food as a love language
And the way you are so selfless and caring that
it pisses me off
Yeah, I'm that way too
The list could go on and on and on
Because I truly am a mini you
And the only thing that bothers me more than
that
Is not being able to share with you how
awesome I think that is sometimes

Our tides are always changing

I wish our push and pull was as in sync
And as beautiful as the connection
Between the moon and the waves

Please, just let me be

I'll be the first to admit that I'm not perfect
But I never get the chance around you
Because you'd always beat me to it
So in the time when I was learning to heal
You constantly reminded me of why I'm broken
Even though you're the one who broke me in the
first place

Shattered mirrors

I shattered the mirror so it would finally be an
accurate reflection
Broken and in pieces
With sharp edges that could cut you if you're not
careful
But if you look closely you can still make out
the image
And you know what
Shattered mirrors still reflect light

I promise I love you

I want so badly to tell you how proud I am of
you
But the letters get jumbled between my brain
and my mouth
And come out as an insult instead
And when I try to tell you I love you
It's like my tongue doesn't know how to
pronounce it
For every grain of sand on the beach
I've thought about telling you these things
But it slips through the broken pieces in my
heart
And grows heavy in my chest
As the love that was meant for you
Turns into anger for myself

Feeding the wrong fire

The stinging in my chest
Are the embers of my past reigniting
As I continue to gaslight myself
I can feel the fire burn the back of my throat
There's a throbbing in my head
And my body aches
But I'm fine

Being the sun means nothing in a world of many galaxies

You told me I was your sun
That I light up your world
You were right here next to me
But your head was in the clouds
I searched the world for you
Only to find you in another galaxy
Where the sun's light never reaches

Not this one too, God

I know God closes doors for a reason
But when you slammed that door in my face
All I wanted to do was rip it back open

Starry eyes

The stars in my eyes
Are from all the times I stared at the sky
Praying for someone like you

Holding on to the good times

It's hard holding onto the good memories
When you know how it all ends

A letter to Love

Dear Love,

You kind of have an RBF

Sincerely,
A girl who just wants to know what all the hype
is about

Old soul

Perhaps the reason I'm so fascinated with the 60s
and 70s is because
It's a time in the world that doesn't know who I
am
A time in the history of the world that will never
see my soul
Bring me back to that time
So I may see how I could've lived differently
Where my heart seems to actually fit the puzzle
And my mind could ease into the fact that I
might just belong

Thief

No matter how much you take from me
It will never fill the gaping hole in your heart

I miss you

I wanted to reach out but you seemed better off
without me
I got scared that so much time had gone by
That you had forgotten about me
I wasn't enough to make you stay
And I'm certainly not enough to bring you back
I don't even know if I'm enough to occupy a
small corner of your mind
Meanwhile, you've completely taken over mine
Everything reminds me of you
Was it really that easy to let go of me?

This one is for my family

You are quite literally my everything
And I'm sorry for the times I treat you like
nothing
My ego can be as blinding as the summer sun
But you are the roots of my tree
I hope to never forget that
May you soon get to see the fruits of my tree
ripen
And feed the many souls I touch

"Do the do"

As the path got darker
My hope wavered with every flicker of my
flashlight
And my voice trembled as I cried for help
And there you were
A steady hand for the stepping stones that felt
like mountains
In those moments
You made trust seem so easy
Your guidance and never-ending kindness
Is something I cherish every morning when I
take my first breath
If you didn't know it before
I am eternally grateful for you

Big impact by small people

When I look at the stars
I'm reminded of how little we are
But when I look at you
I remember how big of an impact we can still
make

Love yourself as your neighbor

The way she was
The way she is
The way she will be
I still love her